Wolverine

Children Book of Fun Facts & Amazing Photos on Animals in Nature - A Wonderful Wolverine Book for Kids aged 3-7

By

Ina Felix

Ina Felix

Copyright © 2015 by Ina Felix

All rights reserved. No part of this book may be used or reproduced in any manner whatsoever without the express written permission of the publisher except for the use of brief quotations in a book review. Image Credits: Royalty free images reproduced under license from various stock image repositories. Under a creative commons licenses.

I am a Wolverine.

They also call me "Gulo gulo" meaning "glutton" in Latin.

That is because I eat a lot.

I am an animal, not a superhero.

Because I don't catch the bad guys.

I live in the forest or a mountain.

They say I look like a bear.

That is because I am large, like a bear.

But actually I am a weasel — a big one at that.

My skin has thick fur that keeps me warm when it is cold.

I have a short legs and small eyes.

I am strong.

I have a sharp claw and powerful jaws.

I use them to fight my enemy and to get food.

I like to travel around and meet my fellow animals.

I love my family; we take care and protect each other.

I am very friendly to everyone unless I am hungry.

I talk to my fellow wolverines most of the time. We share stories with each other.

They think I am scary, but actually I think I am cute!

Sadly, there are only few of us left, so you have to take care of Mother Earth, where we live.

I hope you had fun learning about my family.

Thank you.

Made in the USA
Lexington, KY
10 October 2017